Grieve with Grace

Embarking on the painful journey of grief to rediscover purpose, acceptance, and faith after the loss of a loved one.

SHUNTOYA CHATMAN MSW, LCSW, LISW-CP, DOT-SAP

Copyright © 2022 SHUNTOYA CHATMAN MSW, LCSW, LISW-CP, DOT-SAP

All rights reserved. It is illegal to reproduce, duplicate, or transmit any part of this document in either electronic means or printed format. Copying this publication is strictly prohibited and any replication of this document is not allowed unless with written permission from SHUNTOYA CHATMAN MSW, LCSW, LISW-CP, DOT-SAP.

ISBN: 9798817214253

Dedication

I dedicate this devotion to my first offspring, my angel, Christopher Jr that brought so much joy, laughter, and love into my life at the tender age of 25. The four years of memories we created will forever remain etched on my heart.

When I felt your first kick in my womb, I knew you would be special. My angel, thank you for the opportunity to be your mother. Your physical absence is missed and felt daily, but I know that you are in heaven which gives me comfort. This road of grief has not been easy, but it has been necessary for my growth. Xoxoxo

Acknowledgments

I am nothing without the unconditional love, saving grace, protection, and blessings from my savior, Jesus Christ. Lord, I did not understand this test when this trial occurred early in my life, but with age and wisdom, I have finally arrived at the place of acceptance.

To my grandmothers, the late Dillie Mae Lambert and the late Beatrice Moore, thank you for the legacies that you both left for me to continue.

To my loving and supportive parents, Dorothy and John Jones, I appreciate the sacrifices you both made to help be in the position that I am in today.

To my blood sisters, Kathan Labran and Gelicia Washington, thank you for allowing me to serve as your big sister and encouraging me during this process.

To my spouse, Anthony Chatman, Sr I appreciate you for being by myside as I navigated life, the twist and turns that came unexpectedly.

To my beautiful children, Aubrey and Anthony Jr that inspire me to become a better version of self and love me unconditional, your births have brought me overabundance of joy.

I must acknowledge my sorority/spiritual sisters that have added so much happiness to my life and have been with me during the darkest moments of my life, Marcia Primas, Dr. Joffery Gaymon, Edwina Roberson, Fenita Williams, Tanessa Thomas, and Janetta Vickers. A special shout out to the greatest sorority in the world, Zeta Phi Beta Sorority, Inc especially the ETA XI chapter at Georgia College & State University. I crossed the burning sands twenty plus years ago and I continue to foster the principles of sisterhood, services, scholarship, and finer womanhood.

To the creative editor of this journal, Grace Marie Brown, owner of Pen to Publish I appreciate your guidance on this project.

To my church family at Green Branch CFC, I appreciate the prayers and an assembly that provides teachings which has contributed to my faith walk and taught me the value of having a personal relationship with God.

And lastly, let me thank my ancestors for their laboring that afforded me the opportunities that I have today, I don't take lightly this platform I have been gifted with.

Contents

Introduction	1
Five Stages of Grief	6
Let's Tackle Depression	9
What is Bargaining?	12
Is Denial Acceptable?	15
When Will I Arrive at Acceptance	18
The Importance of Food During Grief	21
Stay Physically Active	24
Sooo…What Do I Do About Work	27
Do I Need a Village	30
So Now I Need a Shrink?	33
Routine Creates Consistency	36
Tell Me More About Self-Care	39
Should I Talk About It or Not?	42
How to Process Dreams	45
Decisions, Decisions, Decisions	48

How Do I Move Forward?   51

Avoid Picking Up Bad Habits   54

Introduction

One thing I have learned on this journey called life is grief is one of the most unavoidable universal rites of passage that we all will encounter. No one can skip this part. It is a path that we will all travel. Your social class, job title, or the amount of money in the bank does not allow any exemptions.

Grief is a God-given emotion that is displayed due to the harsh reality of loss. If you don't believe me read the bible and you will find several accounts of mourning. For example, Jesus grieves the death of Lazarus. Grief can show up as a variety of emotions such as sadness, anger, confusion, etc. Loss is not only associated with physical death, but grief can be experienced due to divorce, the decline in physical health, job loss, or the aging process.

This journal will focus on the physical death of a loved one and how to put the pieces of one's life back together. I am reminded of a quote from the matriarch of my family, the late Dillie Mae Lambert *"There are two things that you will experience on this earth, birth and death."* I want you to use this guide to accept the things that you cannot change. Grief is something that we must become accustomed to because it will happen without notice.

I want this journal to serve as a guide when you have decided to embark on the healing journey. It will offer direction, understanding, and purpose in navigating the troubling waters of loss. I am truly a believer in the statement that pain can birth purpose.

Remember you are not alone and at times it feels like you are on an island by yourself tasked to stay sane. Don't be ashamed to reach out for help and guidance. Help is available in many forms. I believe strength is conveyed by seeking support and being open about one's mental state. No one can read your mind and so verbally the assistance must be acquired.

I have learned through my grief journey that it does not have an end. It is a cycle that can manifest at different seasons of your life with the same intensity when you first experience this emotion. The ups and downs, highs and lows of this process will make you feel as if insanity is near. However, balance can make its way into your life, but it must be desired and invited by you. God will make sure that you will encounter others that may be further along with their healing that can speak life into your situation.

I remember this old but relevant saying *"you won't be the first and you definitely won't be the last."* This quote resonates that what you are experiencing others have been there too. This journey has been traveled by countless others. There are footprints, tire marks, and tears to concur that it is real. Just go on to any social media site and I promise you will find personal accounts of grief. Check the obituary section of the local newspaper. Grief is happening in the U.S. and abroad.

I hope my words and experiences can be refreshing, and somewhat comforting by creating hope for a better day. Be of good cheer, my friend! Joy will come in the morning! The question is do you have the capacity to endure until that time comes? When it comes to using this guide, please don't read it in chronological order. Your mood, thoughts, and the date of the event will be some of the determining factors on how to approach this activity. There is no wrong way to do it.

This journal is a guide to assist you with embracing grief along with navigating the challenges that comes with this journey. I have included Bible scriptures that have been comforting to me and improved my faith walk throughout the years. Please read each verse several times during the day, speak it out loud, and write the verse on sticky notes to facilitate change and heal your wounded heart. Recalling bible verses during moments of overwhelming sadness have encouraged me to get out of the bed, not breakdown in the grocery store, and keep me focus while completing tasks at work.

There is no specific order when it comes to the bible verses, and you can apply any verse when completing the sections in the journal. I have also included in the back of this journal additional blank pages to document thoughts, feelings, conversations that you would like to have one with your loved one, and to draw pictures that resonates with you. There is no time frame to complete the entire journal, I say go with the pace that best fits you and current lifestyle. I don't want you to rush through the different topics to obtain a completion status. Take your time and let the information sink in!

20 Bible Scriptures to Meditate on Daily

- **Psalm 30:5**
- **Exodus 5:2**
- **Nehemiah 8:10**
- **Psalm 119:28**
- **Proverbs 18:10**
- **Isaiah 40:29-31**
- **2nd Corinthians 12:9-10**
- **Ephesians 6:10-11**
- **Psalm 73:26**
- **2nd Corinthians 13:9**

- **Joshua 1:9**
- **Matthew 5:1-4**
- **Revelation 21:4**
- **Psalm 34:18**
- **Psalm 147:3**
- **John 14:1**
- **1 Thessalonians 4:13-14**
- **John 14:27**
- **Isiah 57:1-2**
- **Lamentations 3: 31-32**

Five Stages of Grief

Scripture to Meditate on

_____
_____
_____
_____

This emotional cycle that Dr. Elizabeth Keubler Ross developed was intended for individuals that were transitioning and coming to terms with their array of emotions because of a terminal illness. She realized in her studies how these stages could become applicable to the individuals, family, and friends that also had to witness their loved ones dying.

What I have learned from years of working in the field of mental health as a Social Worker and comforting individuals dealing with grief is that the stages are not as linear or traveled the same. There are still individuals that are unaware of the five stages of Grief. It is important to discuss these stages so you can identify where you may be on this journey.

The five stages of Grief are anger, depression, bargaining, denial, and acceptance. So first let's start with anger.

Anger is a natural emotional response that an individual can express especially when feeling hopeless or afraid concerning the future. Anger will show up like a tsunami wave when you are alone thinking about scenarios or decisions that possibly could have been implemented to change the outcome related to the loss. Anger can surface like a bubbling volcano due to feelings of powerlessness or helplessness when believing that something different could have been done to change the situation. Anger can be inappropriately misdirected at others especially those closest to us when trying to grasp the *Why me??* or *How could this happen?*

There is a need at times to point fingers or place the blame on things or people that in our hearts we know will not change what has occurred. Anger may cause us to question our faith and if this situation that occurred was due to a type of punishment for one's misbehavior. I can also misdirect this anger to myself and create unnecessary suffering to account for the missed opportunities to make a difference. There will be several thoughts that come about that can contribute to the anger lingering and making it difficult to resolve in real-time.

This fire raging in your body can quickly consume you so be careful because it does not take much to initiate the flame. Again, it is important to share with those that we trust one's level of anger along with finding appropriate methods to address it. You need to identify an outlet for this emotion because if it lingers resentment and bitterness will make their home in your heart.

The 3 takeaways for today

1_____

2_____

3_____

Let's Process it

Identify the stage that you are currently experiencing based on your emotional state. What can you do differently moving forward to address this emotion?

_____
_____
_____
_____
_____
_____
_____
_____
_____
_____
_____
_____

Let's Tackle Depression

Scripture to Meditate on

_____
_____
_____
_____

Depression is another response that one can encounter when experiencing grief. It's this overwhelming feeling of sadness that just lingers for days. Time appears to stop because of the lack of motivation to participate in any type of activity. Each day appears to blend into the next. Trying to keep time or track of each day can be difficult to do.

An example of how grief can impact someone is having a heavy blanket placed over the body and left to ponder on thoughts that are filled with despair and doom. The darkness feels inviting and its cloak becomes acceptable.

Numbness will start to set in as one tries to review the information and make sense of the events that transpired. It's like hitting the playback button on a VCR. You will find yourself rewinding information searching for information or clues.

Self-Isolation is a common practice for those that are grieving. The days appear grey without any color. Sleep deprivation can occur during this period of grief. One's sleep pattern is disrupted especially if the loved one was in the home with you or called you at a certain time of the day. Trying to adapt to a new schedule where the contact or interaction with this individual will no longer exist will be difficult for a couple of weeks. Give yourself time when it comes to changing one's schedule or routine.

The confusion, anger, and sadness will cause one to not feel the desire or energy to entertain or converse. It's tough to get out of bed, eat, or sleep some days because of this energy-draining condition. During this period, it's difficult to find joy or understanding when consumed with thoughts concerning our deceased loved ones. The question of Why me? How could this have happened? What could I have done differently? The thoughts that will start to bubble up from the streams of subconsciousness will disrupt your attention span and it will be difficult to complete tasks.

The 3 takeaways for today

1_____

2_____

3_____

Let's Process it

Write out your thoughts on how depression is being displayed especially when it comes to social interaction or sleep. Have you noticed a change in your food intake? Do you lack the motivation to bathe or get out of bed? Describe your thoughts here.

_____
_____
_____
_____
_____
_____
_____
_____
_____
_____
_____
_____
_____
_____
_____
_____
_____
_____
_____
_____
_____

What is Bargaining?

Scripture to Meditate on

_____
_____
_____
_____

Bargaining is a desperate attempt to understand or make sense of the devastation that has impacted one's world. Replaying the last time speaking to the person whether in person or by phone will create mixed emotions. Pleading with God to change the circumstances in return for something valuable such as more time with that person or being less angry are examples of bargaining.

Creating scenarios in one's mind to provide a different outcome to seek temporary relief will occur. Imagine the last moments of the person's life or events that could have taken place can create anger along with disbelief. The playback of conversations with the deceased person or trying to identify ominous signs of death will develop. The frequency of this type of mind game will vary.

I remember asking God that if I had more time with my

son how I would have parent him differently. I would have been more attentive and in tune with his needs. I can still recount the days I would cry out to God for understanding.

Finally, I had to accept that I loved him, and our bond was unbreakable. Being a perfect parent would not have changed this situation or extended his life on this earth. It took years for me to arrive at this conclusion.

The 3 takeaways for today

1_____

2_____

3_____

Let's Process it

Write down the thoughts that appear in your mind when trying to process death? Do these thoughts make you feel guilty? Remember to stick to the facts of the situation.

_____

_____

_____

_____

_____

_____

Is Denial Acceptable?

Scripture to Meditate on

_____
_____
_____
_____

Denial is when you are unable to accept what has occurred. It is an irrational position of disbelief one may encounter in hoping the information shared will be proven wrong. This emotion can occur when one learns of his or her loved one passing or receives the grim news concerning the impending deterioration of the person's physical condition.

Trying to come to the realization or terms of what is happening can be difficult to accomplish. Sometimes one can fall into a dream-like state and be unable to recall the activities he or she participated in the day. The day and events that occur can appear in a fog, blur-like state and this may be the time that short-term memory loss can take place. I feel this is a coping mechanism for the brain to protect us from overly consuming trauma by creating a barricade for the flooding of emotions.

Some individuals won't accept the person has passed until the viewing of the deceased body. This is the information that shocks the person back to reality like an AED used for CPR. Denial can create anger or cause one to point fingers at others in an accusatory fashion in hopes to rationalize the circumstances.

Denial can cause one to mentally replay the events that transpired before the death and make changes to obtain comfort. Denial is a tough place to be, and confusion can also accompany this emotion. Unfortunately, no matter the conclusion one may arrive at it will not change what has occurred. Again, it is difficult to stay when this emotion may appear. It can show up before depression or bargaining. What is important is the ability to recognize the emotion.

The 3 takeaways for today

1_____

2_____

3_____

Let's Process it

Write down why accepting this loss is difficult and share this with someone close to you this perspective. Develop a daily positive affirmation on how to move away from this thought process.

When Will I Arrive at Acceptance?

Scripture to Meditate on

_____
_____
_____
_____

Acceptance This is a biggie. It takes time, I mean years for some to come to the place of acceptance. It is almost like a type of surrender, waving the white flag. So, I guess you would like to know how this occurs. Let me say this, it is not easy. It is possible for those that no longer want to bargain or try to consciously change what has happened.

One must arrive at the realization that his/her loved one is no longer in present form. The pointing of fingers and trying to find someone to blame for what has taken place will no longer be the focus. This is the step I believe is more like a resolution. Now I would be remiss to suggest that at this stage the pain will magically go away. The pain is there but it is bearable. This equates to I can move forward with my life and no longer allow the past to keep me bounded.

To arrive at this stage, will take some serious work such as enrolling in therapy or developing healthy coping skills to continue maneuvering the obstacles through life. I have realized that I could have done nothing different to change the deceased person's path. It also requires relieving self of the responsibility of keeping this person here, alive. It also recognizes that a higher power is now in control. Shame, blame, guilt, and anger are slowly starting to dissolve. Now the color when it comes to one's surroundings has returned. I am no longer seeing objects in black or white hues. My ability to stay present and not revert to the past is consistent.

When our deceased loved ones' birthdays come, no longer is the dark cloud hovering over us. We can smile more often and recall the happy memories created with our deceased loved ones. Their absences are still noticeable, but now we can go about our daily living tasks with minimal tears. Peace and a glimpse of joy are returning to my life. I can find more things to smile about.

The 3 takeaways for today

1_____

2_____

3_____

Let's Process it

Write a letter to the deceased loved one sharing how acceptance has come and the changes that one has noticed since arriving at this stage. Read this letter to at least one trusted person/companion. Keep this letter and read it during the anniversary of the person's death to confirm one's healing journey.

The Importance of Food During Grief

Scripture to Meditate on

_____
_____
_____
_____

Nutrition is so important to understand during this difficult season of life. I promise you that eating will be the last task that one will be concerned with or take priority. I believe the nerves, emotional state, and physical being are impacted by grief. These elements can contribute to loss of appetite, nausea, and food tasting bland.

How can one eat when tears are constantly running down your face? So, food no longer has significance as we try to process all that is happening. However, we understand the necessity of food when it comes to one's endurance and strength. I know you will get tired of family and friends pushing, almost forcing you to eat.

I would suggest finding foods that can provide nutritional

value as you deal with all the emotions that one is experiencing. I can attest to losing several pounds when I was grieving because I did not have my mind on food nor was I hungry. I had great support that understood my position but did bring items that could help me prevent dehydration or a quick trip to the ER.

I would suggest simple snacks that don't require preparation such as yogurt, applesauce, smoothies, or nuts would be easy to digest. Soups and herbal teas are great sources when it comes to liquids.

During the beginning of my grief journey, I could not eat because of all the emotions that I was experiencing. A close friend purchased several cans of Boost which I was able to consume daily. I was so grateful for this kind gesture. Try your best to monitor your intake of food and this can be done by the number of times you go to the bathroom. I know this sounds very personal, but I am trying to give you the most realistic perspective that I can.

Overeating can also occur during this difficult season because comfort cannot achieve in the physical form. Become aware of the frequency of eating more foods that are packed in high calories, sugar, and saturated in fat. Emotional eating can create more health problems later and comprise one physical status.

The 3 takeaways for today

1_____

2_____

3_____

Let's Process it

What is your nutritional intake such as liquids and solid foods? Did you eat breakfast? Lunch? Dinner? If so, write it down and continue to monitor this situation daily. Also, obtain an accountability partner to remind you to drink or eat throughout the day.

_____
_____
_____
_____
_____
_____
_____
_____
_____
_____
_____
_____
_____
_____
_____
_____
_____
_____

Stay Physically Active

Scripture to Meditate on

_____
_____
_____
_____

Physical Activity can be helpful when it comes to managing your emotions. Endorphins are released in your bloodstream when participating in an activity that increases one's heart rate. It can also assist with regulating your mood.

Now, I am not suggesting for you go join a gym and start lifting heavyweight. I can only speak on experience and how this activity saved me from sitting in my home with my thoughts. There were times during the day when I was alone. Going to the gym was like an escape for me and a way to allow the sweat pouring from my face to cleanse me in a sense.

I feel it is important to find ways to decrease stress, and muscle tension, and productively manage thoughts. Taking a walk, sitting in a park, and biking through the neighborhood can be good interventions in releasing muscle tension. If one is left with only thoughts, it can create an impact on the body and spirit. I have always heard that an idle mind can be the playground for the devil.

Now don't get me wrong. Some moments being still and quiet can be effective, especially when preparing for bedtime or waking up in the morning. There is plenty of research on this topic to enforce the importance of incorporating some type of physical activity during the day.

The 3 takeaways for today

1_____

2_____

3_____

Let's Process it

How motivated are you to begin at least one physical activity? Find an accountability partner to accompany you on the walk or bike ride for inspiration and consistency. Document the number of days during the week that you participate in an activity and the duration.

_____

_____

Sooo...what do I do about work?

Scripture to Meditate on

_____
_____
_____
_____

Employment is another area that I want to point out that normally people don't discuss. It can be very difficult to return to work after experiencing a loss. I have heard of this clique statement; work keeps the mind busy. The problem with this theory is that most time it doesn't, and I have countless feedback from clients seeking grief counseling to prove this concept is false. If your mind is wandering and occupied with mixed emotions, it does not change when returning to work.

Depending on the nature of the job duties, I would suggest not resuming after a month of experiencing loss. I can hear people shouting, how I am going to pay my bills??? Well, there are ways to receive assistance such as using annual leave if provided at the job. I would highly recommend speaking to your HR representative for guidance if any type of financial assistance program is available if the annual leave is not an option.

During my grief journey, I took a month off and was better prepared to face the staff along with being in the environment. I want to share that at times I would become emotional at work, but my colleagues were very understanding along with support. They noticed when I would not come around as often as I did in the past or eat alone. They were very observant and tried to find ways to get to smile or be comfortable in this space.

The 3 takeaways for today

1_____

2_____

3_____

Let's Process it

Ask yourself, am I ready to return to work? How many days off should I give myself before I return? What type of accommodations should I request so my transition can be easier? More breaks? Extended lunch hours? Changing my work hours?

Do I Need a Village?

Scripture to Meditate on

_____
_____
_____
_____

A support system is a necessity to have or create when embarking on the grief journey. I am not asking for you to go out and make new friends. It will be important to lean on close family members or friends to help you with putting the pieces back together when it comes to your personal life.

After the funeral, you will need someone to talk to help process the events that occurred. Sometimes you just need someone to listen and not judge when discussing your loved one. Having a concerned and sincere person to check on you by phone or text can be helpful.

There are social media groups that you can join that can provide support or care. Facebook is a great place to start. I would suggest searching for grief support groups. Online support groups are growing and easily accessible. There are virtual groups that meet online to support grievers. There are websites such as Compassionate Friends that one can access with resources such as books, readings, and local chapters to join for in-person support. Local churches can be another resource when it comes to supporting especially in a group setting.

Don't be quick to turn down assistance when offered by others. No one is asking for you to be strong and appear unphased by what has occurred. It takes courage to let someone know that you need an extra hug, listening ear, or visit to help the day go easier.

The 3 takeaways for today

1_____

2_____

3_____

Let's Process it

Where can I go to access support outside my family and friends? Please write down options that are available in your local community. I have included some options to explore in the resources section of this journal.

So Now I Need a Shrink?

Scripture to Meditate on

_____
_____
_____
_____

Therapy is a vital resource that will be essential when it comes to healing to access. There is so much that you can learn and process by working with a licensed mental health professional during this season of your life.

I remember when I first entered therapy, and I did not know what to expect. My grief was so painful I knew that I needed a third party, neutral person to help me make sense of the things I was experiencing at the time. Just having someone to listen to and try not to make you feel ashamed of one's emotional state was life-changing. I was able to disclose to her the shame and guilt I felt with this loss. She was so kind, understanding, patient, and resourceful. The information that she shared changed my perspective when it came to the loss.

At the time I was blaming myself for the death of my child and she was able to help me change this narrative. Therapy provided me with coping tools that I was unaware of until seeking this type of help. I also utilized this outlet to share my fears, tears, and anger without any corrections. Therapy helped me as I walked through the stages of grief.

The 3 takeaways for today

1_____

2_____

3_____

Let's Process it

If you are employed, please contact your employer's HR department or HR representative to request an employee assistance program. If not please search via the internet on therapist directories such as clinicians of color, black girls of therapy, and psychology today for self-pay and/or insurance payment options. Write down the name and date of the initial appointment with the selected therapist.

_____

_____

_____

Routine Creates Consistency

Scripture to Meditate on

_____
_____
_____
_____

Daily Routine is something that will take time to reinstitute. Grief will impact time in a manner as if it stops or starts to move noticeably slowly. The days can start to blend, and it can become difficult to determine which day one is presently in. I have heard people say when they learn of their loved ones passing or witnessed their transition that "time stood still."

Confusion, which is an emotion caused by grief can change one's normal habits. I can recall where I would take naps during the day and be up most of the night. This is because my mind was constantly bombarded with irrational thoughts and night became the time, I dreaded the most because of the stillness that existed. The distractions in my environment were minimal at night and this became the time that I would think the most out loud. It would take several months before I was able to resume a normal 7 hours of sleep without waking up during the night. The dark was disruptive and no longer welcomed, as I had to find ways to incorporate light in my bedroom by leaving the TV on or using a nightlight.

Some individuals may be convinced to take a sleep aid type of medication over the counter or from a physician. I would say proceed with caution because these medications can create more problems, especially side effects. I would recommend not utilizing them as a permanent solution when experiencing poor sleep hygiene. I would say be patient and when the body along with the mind starts to wind down, then your sleep pattern will improve. Trust the process!

The 3 takeaways for today

1_____

2_____

3_____

Let's Process it

Choose a routine to focus on such as bedtime or morning. Write down how you will go about following through with this concept and the perceived benefits when it comes to incorporating the designated tasks related to the selected routine.

Tell Me More About Self-Care

Scripture to Meditate on

_____
_____
_____
_____

Self-Care is the new buzzword when it comes to improving one's wellbeing. Of course, I had to incorporate this into the journal. I believe in its importance and regular implementation to manage grief. This practice is so important because of the rollercoaster ride that one's emotions will embark on. Self-care and the interventions to embody this principle will help revitalize, heal, and improve the mindset along with the body.

It is important to be intentional about doing something good for you. I know that at times guilt will try to convince you that it is not ideal to show love to yourself. I promise you that taking one step will produce benefits along with relief. Examples of this activity could include bubble baths, pedicures, getting your hair done, or going to the spa to receive the back massage that you have dreamed about. I say do it and don't allow judgment from others or guilt to prevent you from this healthy practice. This too can be an outlet to release the pain that you have kept suppressed within.

This is in no way a selfish act and don't let anyone try to convince you of this. This act is not dishonoring your deceased loved one. Hopefully, as you continue to become comfortable with self-care it will become second nature and regular practice.

The 3 takeaways for today

1_____

2_____

3_____

Let's Process it

Plan a day of self-care with an accountability partner if needed. There will be tears and probably some level of discomfort but push through it. Write down how you felt after completing the activity and what you learned about yourself for completing this important step.

_____

_____

Should I Talk About it or Not?

Scripture to Meditate on

_____
_____
_____
_____

Discussing the Loss can be so difficult to share with others. People can at times be unconsciously ignorant or uncaring by probing for information when it comes to the circumstances that contributed to our loved one's passing. Clients have shared with me how individuals would inappropriately stop to inquire about the deceased loved one while he or she was shopping in the grocery store or out paying the gas bill. Bringing up or trying to recall this information can be triggering and retraumatizing to those that are mourning.

Please use your voice to speak up kindly but firmly advising the inquiring individual that you are not in the position to discuss the matter. Don't feel forced or pushed to revisit information that may cause you to become emotionally vulnerable. Will that person stick around to console you after disrupting your concentration and mood? It is up to you to discuss specifics concerning the events that were connected to the loved one's passing and that could be months or even years before I share. Take your time when recalling information during conversations that you are not prepared for nor have the energy to engage in.

The 3 takeaways for today

1_____

2_____

3_____

Let's Process it

Prepare your speech on how you will respond to individuals inquiring about the incident. Don't let anyone force you to speak about the details of the incident. Sometimes recalling information can be retraumatizing. Let's write it down.

_____

_____

_____

_____

How to Process Dreams

Scripture to Meditate on

_____
_____
_____
_____

Dreams and how they come to fruition can vary from person to person. I have heard that dreaming is the gateway to the world of unconsciousness. However, I have personal encounters from my journey and clients encountering their deceased loved ones during dreams.

My grandmother discussed experiencing her deceased spouse and child visiting her while she was asleep on many occasions. I finally was able to experience this phenomenon myself and I am so glad that I did.

Now I want to caution you that not everyone will have this encounter. This does not suggest that your loved one is indifferent to your suffering nor desire to return to you. I cannot say why some have these dream-like encounters and others don't. I did not wish for it to take place. I can still recall the dream as if it happened yesterday and how my son visited me with much joy and peace. I felt that maybe this interaction was orchestrated by God to encourage my healing journey. I am so grateful for this chance to say goodbye I felt symbolic. I have not received any more visits or dreams concerning my child since then. So yes, supernatural things can occur in the spiritual realm but having an open mind is critical to the experience.

The 3 takeaways for today

1_____

2_____

3_____

Let's Process it

If you had an encounter with your loved one in a dream, immediately write down what happened. Don't review the information until the next day. How did you feel after this incident?

Will you tell someone about this experience?

_____
_____
_____
_____
_____
_____
_____

Decisions, Decisions, Decisions

Scripture to Meditate on

_____
_____
_____
_____

Decisions are something that I would suggest to not be the focus or urge especially when the grief is new, fresh. I am aware that decisions such as funeral home arrangements, expenses, life insurance, etc will need to be addressed. There is no avoiding them unless you have a trusted individual that can stand in the gap while you are mourning.

I am speaking of my making big expensive purchases or changing job positions. Mentally because your emotional state is so raw and vulnerable, decisions can be made based on your current state. You may not factor in the consequences or outcomes when it comes to one's decision-making capacity.

As a therapist, I have encountered people that made rash decisions without discussing these plans with trusted individuals to later regret rushing knowing they were ill-prepared for this duty. I would suggest waiting at least six months after the loss to decide if putting off the decision was done in good judgment. And if it is worth wanting then the wait should not make any difference.

The 3 takeaways for today

1_____

2_____

3_____

Let's Process it

What are your short-term goals that can be achieved in six months? A Year? Why working towards these goals should wait should be outlined along with each goal whether it is concerning my career, going back to school, or relocating to another state or city.

How Do I Move Forward?

Scripture to Meditate on

_____
_____
_____
_____

Moving Forward is a step that I will not assign as being the last thing to endure but it will suggest that some progress has been made in the healing journey. Remember grief is ongoing and it does not end. The pain will still be present, and the absence of our loved ones will still be felt.

However, I hope that at this place in the path you have realized certain things that are considered absolutes. Grief will cause us to park when it comes to life and enjoying the fruit of it. I am suggesting that hopefully, you will acquire the strength to put the car in drive and start the journey of rediscovery.

Unfortunately, our loved ones will not return. Our lives will never be the same. The tears will still flow but not as frequently as when we first encountered this situation. You will change mentally and spiritually but hopefully for the best. The colors in the leaves and flowers will return with a vibrancy that one has missed or gone because of one's mental status. Be encouraged my friend, the end is not near. Soar and live life abundantly!

The 3 takeaways for today

1_____

2_____

3_____

Let's Process it

I would encourage you to go back and review the information documented in this journal so you can visually note the work that has been done. Hopefully, this activity will provide relief and hope for the future.

_____
_____
_____
_____
_____
_____
_____
_____
_____

Avoid Picking Up Bad Habits

Scripture to Meditate on

_____
_____
_____
_____

Unfortunately, those that don't have access to the resources, services, or supports available can make an unconscious, illogical decision to find temporary relief in places or things that are unhealthy. Alcohol, drugs, gambling, and other risky behaviors can create a mirage of hope or escape for individuals when it comes to the grips that grief can have in your personal life. The pain and loss can be so intense that a person with a broken spirit will succumb to the temptations that exist in our communities. However, it is important to understand that these choices will not create peace but negative consequences that we may not be prepared to accept.

These habits will increase the chaos that you may experience by inviting more drama into your world. So, let's make a personal commitment to not seek destructive ways to numb the pain. We must endure the pain to heal. Adding more problems to our lives will not change the circumstances. Self-destructive behavior will do more harm than good. It will prevent you from experiencing the fullness of things life has to offer.

The 3 takeaways for today

1_____

2_____

3_____

Let's Process it

Find a song that can encourage you in the weakest time in your life. Recite, write down the lyrics, and if available watch the video for the song. Allow this song to become etched into your conscious and heart to recall when needed. My favorite song to listen to when I was feeling discouraged or tearful was by Kirk Family and God's Property "He'll Take the Pain Away." Listening to this song in the present still can cause tears to come because of the pain I have experienced and the growth achieved because of my loss. For encouragement, creating a playlist was vital in supporting my healing journey.

_____

_____

Resources

- Please contact 911 or the local emergency room if you or someone you know are experiencing suicidal thoughts or wanting to harm others.
- Compassionate Friends https://www.compassionatefriends.org National Headquarters 877-969-0010
- Griefshare https://www.griefshare.org/
- My Grief Angels https://www.mygriefangels.org/
- AARP Grief and Loss resources https://www.aarp.org/caregiving/grief-loss-end-of-life/?cmp=RDRCT-bf1da46e-20210730
- National Widowers Organization https://nationalwidowers.org/
- American Foundation for Suicide Prevention https://afsp.org/
  National Line 800-273-8255
- Grief Center https://icwb.com/grief-center
- Social Media support group https://www.griefanonymous.com/facebook-groups/

- Grief in Common
  https://www.griefincommon.com/

- Tommy's https://www.tommys.org/baby-loss-support/stillbirth-information-and-support/coping-grief-after-loss-baby-parents

- Therapists Directory
  https://www.therapyincolor.org/
  https://www.cliniciansofcolor.org/find-a-therapist/
  https://therapyforblackgirls.com/
  https://www.psychologytoday.com/us
  https://www.therapyden.com/

- Hospice Foundation of America
  https://hospicefoundation.org/Grief-%281%29

- http://www.Tenderheartssupport.com

- My Grief Instagram Profile
  Grieve w/ Grace (@grieve_with_grace

- Podcast
  This Too Shall Suck: A Fresh Perspective on Grief
  The Grief Coach: Conversation about Life and Death

About the Author

Shuntoya Chatman is a Licensed Clinical Social Worker with more than 12 years of experience in the human service/social work field. Shuntoya Chatman earned a bachelor's degree in Community Health and a master's degree in public administration from Georgia College & State University.

She also earned a master's degree in Social Work from Valdosta State University. She is the owner of Wholistic Counseling Services, LLC. She is married to her spouse, Anthony Sr, and the mother of three children, Aubrey, Anthony Jr, and (Christopher Jr, my angel).

She is currently self-employed and provides telehealth therapy along with contractual work for various national employee assistance programs. She enjoys working with clients from all walks of life that may be dealing with symptoms of grief, addiction, and trauma.

For more information, her website address is www.mywholisitccounselingservices.com Her IG and Facebook accounts @WholisticWayTherapy.

Notes and Reflections

Made in the USA
Monee, IL
30 June 2022